GETTING GROWING:
A Beginner's Guide to Container Gardening Basics

Table of Contents

Introduction

Conclusion

INTRODUCTION

Welcome to container gardening! Using containers is a great way to get a garden growing in a small space, a space where you otherwise wouldn't be able to grow any garden at all. You can grow fresh tomatoes on your patio or beautiful, blooming flowers on your apartment balcony.

Container gardens have many advantages over traditional gardens. Container gardens are easier to manage, and their growing environment is easier to control. Soil temperatures are easier to regulate, and planters can be quickly covered to avoid early and late frosts and extend the growing season. Weeds, the bane of the traditional gardener, are practically nonexistent in a container garden. Also, with the popularity of container gardening, several plant varieties have been bred for small space gardens. There are patio varieties of sweet corn, carrots, and cucumbers.

Container gardens are a great place for beginners to learn the art of gardening, and likely you're reading this beginning guide because you are, in fact, a beginning gardener. This gardening handbook is the perfect place to start learning the basics of container gardening. We'll discuss different types of containers and other garden equipment you'll need to get started. We'll also talk about the best types of plants for containers and how to take care of them. When you finish reading this book, you'll know (among many other things):

- How to design your garden to best meet your gardening goals (Chapter 1).
- The pros and cons of ceramic, clay, plastic, wood, and stone containers (Chapter 2).
- The best soil to use in your container garden (Chapter 2).
- How to select the best plants for your container garden (Chapter 3).
- How to transplant, seed-start, and direct sow your plants (Chapter 4).
- Best water and fertilizing practices for your container garden (Chapter 5).
- How to prevent pests and plant disease. (Chapter 5).
- How to handle pests and plant diseases should the problem arise (Chapter 5).
- The best places to go for local garden help. (Conclusion)

I grew up in a family of gardeners, so I've been gardening, in some capacity, all my life. Along the way, I've learned several helpful garden tricks that I pass along in each of the chapters. I highlight easy ways to cut garden costs. I also provide a few simple solutions to improving container drainage along with organic options to pest and disease control. I'll let you know why you should avoid using certain containers in certain locations, and even avoid using some containers altogether. The information is presented in an entertaining, jargon-free manner. Container gardening is meant to be fun. Reading about container gardening should be a little entertaining, too.

So, without further ado, it's time to enter the world of container gardening. Read on, jot down a few notes (if you're into that sort of thing), and study up. No, there won't be a test at the end. Your blooming garden with happy, green plants will let you know you got an 'A'.

CHAPTER 1
BEFORE YOU START:
THINGS TO CONSIDER BEFORE GETTING
GROWING

Adding a seed to a container filled with soil, plus a little water and sunlight equals plant, right?

Well, yes, actually. That is the basic idea. But, to get the best end product, say a tomato plant that actually produces tomatoes, you have to choose the right container and the right soil. You have to put your plant in an area where it gets the right amount of sunlight and give your plant the right amount of water.

What is "right" for your garden is largely going to depend on the type of garden you plan on creating. Maybe you just want to liven up your apartment's balcony with a few hanging baskets of geraniums. Maybe you'd like to grow a few pots of basil and oregano on your kitchen counter, so you have easy access to fresh herbs on spaghetti night. Or, maybe, salsa-extraordinaire that you are, you want to grow fresh tomatoes and jalapeños, but your backyard has been commandeered by the kids' swing set, the dog's toys, and your husband's production-sized grill.

Every garden's needs are going to vary depending on the location of the garden, the scope of the garden, and the gardener's goals. Before you start planting, consider the following:

Where will your container garden be located?

- What type of space are you using for your garden? An apartment balcony? A townhouse patio? A backyard?

  Be mindful of any restrictions on your growing space. If your garden will be on a balcony, plant weight may be an issue. If you're using the small backyard your children routinely play in, you might want to avoid plants that attract a lot of bees.

- Will your garden be in a sunny space? A shady space? How many hours of sunlight will your garden receive daily?

  Keep in mind, most vegetable plants require a minimum of six hours of sunlight per day while some flowers need at least partial shade. The amount of sunlight your garden receives will dictate the types of plants you can get to grow.

- What type of climate do you live in? Is it hot? Cool? Humid? Dry? Rainy? Windy? Does your summer temperature top out at 80°, or is 105° nothing to panic about?

  There is a plant for every climate. You can grow peas in Texas and Colorado, but if you live in Texas, you need to choose a variety that's heat resistant, like Zinfandels.
  Being aware of your climate's quirks will help you choose the plants that will grow instead of...well...the plants that won't.

  Climate can also affect the type of growing containers you'll need to use. If you live in a particularly rainy area, you want planters with good drainage. If the wind is constantly blowing, you need bottom-heavy pots to keep plants from tumbling over.

■ When is the growing season in your region? When is the last frost? The first frost? If you live in a hot climate, when do temperatures peak?

Your growing season will determine what you can plant and when you can plant it. If you live in the Pacific Northwest and want to grow tomatoes, choose a variety with a quick production time, like Early Girl. If you live in the South, heat-intolerant lettuce has to be planted in time for a spring harvest.

If you live in Hawaii, you can pretty much plant anything you want all year around, and the rest of us resent you terribly (more so for living in Hawaii than for your advantageous gardening climate).

What Is the Scope of Your Container Garden?

- What is the size of the garden you're planning? How many containers will you be using? Just one planter? Two or three? More?

  If you're a beginning gardener (likely since you're reading this guide), I recommend starting off small. Try growing a few different plants in just two or three containers and see how things go (or grow). You can always expand your garden after you've gotten your first plants going (or growing).

- What plants are you trying to grow? Ornamental flowers? Food producing vegetables? Specifically, what types of flowers? What types of vegetables?

  Identifying what you want to plant will help you zero in on varieties that grow best in your climate and avoid ones that don't.

- How long do you plan on living where you're living? Is your garden a one season experiment in a temporary home or part of a larger landscaping scheme in a permanent one?

  Consider your living arrangement when you're planning your garden budget. If you're in a place you won't reside in for long, like an apartment, know that plants and containers can be a pain to move and are often left behind or passed along to neighbors.

What are Your Goals as a Gardener?

- How much time do you want to spend gardening?

  Some plants will thrive with little attention. The ficus on my back patio keeps growing as long as I keep it in a sunny place and give it an occasional splash of water. Other plants are a bit more time-intensive. For best results, tomato plants need to be pruned, routinely fertilized, and kept on strict watering schedules.

Choose plants with maintenance levels that match the gardening time commitment you're willing to make. Plan your garden to fit your lifestyle rather than the other way around.

- How often are you away from home? Do you have a willing friend or partner who will take over watering duties while you're gone?

  If I go on a weeklong vacation, I know my ficus will survive until I return. I also know my cucumbers will be dead unless I make arrangements to have them watered in my absence.

  If you take frequent trips, you may want to consider drought-tolerant and low maintenance plants.

- How much money are you willing to part with to get started?

  There is a container garden for every budget. Figure out what you're willing to spend now and stick to that amount.

  For your first container garden, I'd advise spending less rather than more. Have fun and experiment a bit with your early gardening efforts and save heavy financial investments for when you're a more seasoned grower.

Identifying the location of your garden, scope of your project, and your goals as a gardener now will payoff immensely when you start purchasing the items you need for your new container garden. You'll know exactly which plants and products you need and why. You can set a gardening budget and stick to it, and you're less likely to be glamoured by gardening products that just won't work for you, a fate that tempts the most experienced of gardeners.

Yes, that Bird of Paradise is gorgeous.

No, it's not going to grow in your outdoor, New England garden.

Mine sure didn't.

Chapter 2
Getting Equipped:
The Dirt on Container Gardening Gear

There are some items you're going to have to acquire before you can start your container garden. First, and most obviously:

Containers

There are a wide variety of containers you can use to get your garden growing. All of them have positives and negatives, and the type of container you choose will depend on the needs of your garden. Here is a list of the more common containers you'll encounter along with a few of the pros and cons of each:

- **Ceramic Pots**

  These glazed containers come in a variety of colors, shapes, and sizes. Ceramic pots can be a slightly pricier option than other containers, but with proper care, they hold up well through several seasons.

  Ceramic pots can cause plants to become waterlogged as many have only a single hole for drainage. If you're planning on using ceramic pots, try to purchase those with more than one drainage port.

  Pros: Variety of choice, durable
  Cons: More expensive, can cause drainage issues

- **Terra Cotta (Clay) Pots**

  Like ceramic pots, terra cotta pots are available in many shapes and sizes, but they tend to be cheaper. If you're crafty, these clay planters can be painted any color you desire; I even had a friend who BeDazzled hers.

  Terra cotta pots are unglazed, so they can become water stained, and their porous surface can sap water from the soil, so you might find yourself watering your plants more frequently. Terra cotta pots tend to chip and break more easily, and they're prone to cracking when soil freezes.

  Pros: Cheaper option, design friendly
  Cons: Less durable, require more frequent watering

- **Plastic Pots**

  Plastic pots are a cost-efficient option and available in many sizes, shapes, and colors. Plastic pots let you avoid the drainage issues of ceramic pots as extra drainage holes can easily be drilled into a plastic container's base.

  Plastic pots tend to break down quickly and usually last just a single season. Also, you may need to use lighter colored pots in high sun areas. Black or dark-colored plastic tends to overheat soil which can damage plant roots.

Pros: Low cost, better drainage
Cons: Break down quickly, soil heating concerns

■ Wood Containers

Costs vary on wood containers, but they can be had on the cheap. They can be purchased ready-made or in a DIY kit. If you're particularly handy, you can probably build a wood planter yourself. Always use wood planters made with untreated lumber as treated-lumber chemicals can leach into your plants and vegetables.

Wood containers provide good drainage and keep soil evenly heated. Wood planters are fairly durable with proper maintenance, but they do require more care than other containers to ensure longevity as wood containers are susceptible to wood rot, insect damage, and weathering.

Pros: Provide a good plant environment, low cost options available
Cons: May be unsuitable for vegetable plants, require greater maintenance

■ Metal Containers

Can I share a secret with you? I have a deep and undying loathing of metal containers. I'll admit they are attractive and often cost friendly. But, metal containers do not drain properly, heat the soil to boiling temperatures, and can be prone to rust. Avoid using antique metal planters as they can contain lead.

If you do plan on using metal containers, I highly advise using them as a shell or cache pot for plastic planters.

Pros: Aesthetically appealing, lower cost
Cons: Drainage problems, overheat soil, durability issues

■ Stone Containers

Stone containers are incredibly attractive and age extremely well. They're also incredibly expensive and extremely heavy, so they may be more suitable as permanent garden features rather than used in transient container gardens.

Stone containers regulate soil temperature and drainage exceptionally well.
Weathering gives stone containers character, but it's important to maintain the stone properly so it doesn't chip. The heft of these containers makes them untenable for many balcony gardens where weight restrictions may come into play.

Pros: Provide a good plant environment, age beautifully
Cons: Expensive, heavy, may be unsuitable for balcony gardens

■ Other Options

There are, of course, other container options than those listed here. And, those containers also have their pros and cons. Hanging baskets, for example, are cheap, lightweight, and a great space saving option. But, they dry out quickly in hot or windy environments (and even quicker in hot, windy environments).

If you're creative, the sky is the limit on containers for your garden. You can use coffee cans or plastic buckets, milk containers or old water bottles. I once used a wooden wine box from a vineyard, and I've seen plants grown in old boots and rubber galoshes. If you're on a tight garden budget, repurposing old items is a great way to cut costs.

A Few Other Container Considerations

- **Size:** The bigger the plant you plan on growing, the bigger the container you're going to need.

- **Color:** Darker colored containers, especially of the plastic variety, will keep soil temperatures higher. Too much heat can damage plant roots and upset the soil's nutrient balance, so be wary of keeping dark pots in full sun, especially in already hot climates.

  Of course, the flip-side of this equation is also true. If you need to add a little heat to your soil because you have a shady garden or live in a cooler climate, invest in black or dark pots.

- **Weight:** Ceramic, terra cotta, and stone containers are naturally going to be weightier pots, especially when filled with soil and plants and water.

If your garden will be on a balcony, confirm any weight restrictions before you get started. If you live in a windy area, you may need heavier pots to keep your plants from blowing over. If you have a windy balcony, you can make plastic pots bottom heavy by layering a base of small stones beneath your potting soil.

Soil

Potting soil, potting soil, potting soil.

It's important, so I'll mention it again.

Potting soil.

Since you're growing a container garden, you need soil engineered for containers. If you're on a budget, soil is likely going to be your priciest outlay, so try and come to terms with that now. Don't be tempted by cheaper garden or top soil. It just won't work for containers. It doesn't drain property and will leave your plants water-logged and unable to establish roots. You'll have inexpensive soil but very dead plants.

Still tempted by a cheaper option? Okay, I'll give you one, but straight-up potting soil would still work better. But, if it's this or nothing, you can stretch your potting soil by mixing it with equal amounts of peat moss and sand.

When purchasing potting soil, pay attention to labels. Some potting soils are better for houseplants, some for roses, and some for vegetables. These mixes are fertilized for the plants they're advertising, so be sure to pick the potting soil that's best for your garden.

Your plants will thank you.

Other Gardening Aids

These items aren't necessarily must-haves, but they are nice-to-haves:

- Gardening gloves
- Garden trowel
- Spray bottles
- Pruning shears
- Soil moisture meter
- Watering can

Chapter 3
Picking Your Crop:
Choosing Plants for Your Garden

The most common question of new container gardeners is, "What plants can I grow?"

The answer is, "Well, pretty much all of them."

If a plant grows in the ground, it will also grow in a container, provided the container is big enough to sustain the plant's root system, and the plant is given the right amount of water and nutrients. Some plants, however, do grow better in containers than others. Bush beans grow a little better than pole beans, and Early Girl tomatoes grow better than Big Boys. When deciding on what plants to grow, consider:

- Most small flowering plants (such as geraniums, trailing ivies, salvias, mums, and pansies, among many, many others) do quite well in container gardens.

- Herbs, like basil, oregano, rosemary, thyme, or sage, also grow very well in containers.

- Annuals are plants with a single season growth cycle and usually have to be replanted each year (though annuals may drop seeds and occasionally reseed themselves in your garden). Perennials are plants that survive multiple seasons.

  Container gardens are a great place to plant annuals, and annuals will grow in most climates. You can also use perennials, but many perennials are region specific, so be sure to choose perennials that will grow in your area.

  Most gardeners use a mix: perennials that return year after year and a rotating crop of annuals to add variety to their garden.

- The most common vegetables grown in containers are snap beans, cherry tomatoes, lettuce, peppers, chard, peas, pickling cucumbers, broccoli, red potatoes, and summer squash. But, all vegetable plants are possible with the right sized container.

- Certain varieties of vegetables have been bred for container and small-space gardens, like Small Fry tomatoes, Spacemaster cucumbers, On Deck hybrid corn, and Half Long carrots. Look for plant labels like "space saver" and "patio pick."

- In reality, all vegetable plants are fair game for container gardens. In practice, smaller varieties usually work better as even they need at least a 5 gallon container to grow in. But, if you have your heart set on growing watermelons or pumpkins it can be done: you just need a very large container space to grow them in.

- Some plants, like peas, cucumbers, and pole beans, can be trained to grow on a trellis to further save garden space.

Here is a list of common annuals, perennials, herbs, and vegetables for container gardens. Many of these are good plants to start with, but this list is by no means all-inclusive. If you live in California and want to try growing artichokes, go for it!

Common Perennials for Container Gardens

Please note: Strictly classifying plants as either annuals or perennials can be a bit tricky. Different varieties of the same plant can be annual, perennial, or even biennial (a plant with a two year growth cycle). Some plants, such as Esperanza or Black-Eyed Susans, can behave either as an annual or perennial depending on the climate it's grown in. I've classified the following flowers in their more common category.

- Ferns
- Salvia
- Bougainvillea
- Columbine
- Shasta Daisy
- Busy Lizzie
- Peonies
- Lavender
- Esperanza
- Primrose
- Pansy (pansies are often used as annuals)
- Begonia
- Ivies
- Mums

Common Annuals for Container Gardens

- Sweet Pea
- Morning Glory
- Zinnia
- Geranium
- Marigold
- Oxalis
- Snapdragon
- Petunia
- Heliotrope
- Fuchsia
- Foxglove
- Forget-Me-Not
- Larkspur

- Nasturtium

Common Herbs for Container Gardens

- Basil
- Oregano
- Parsley
- Dill
- Rosemary
- Thyme
- Cilantro
- Chives
- Tarragon
- Marjoram
- Lemon Balm
- Sage
- Mint

Common Vegetables for Container Gardens

- Tomatoes (cherry or small bush varieties)
- Beans (bush varieties work best, pole beans will need to be staked)
- Peppers (Sweet, Anaheim, Jalapeños, Poblano)
- Radishes
- Cucumbers (pickling or patio varieties)
- Corn (container hybrids)
- Carrots (petite varieties)
- Lettuce
- Broccoli
- Chard
- Strawberries (okay, not a vegetable but will grow in a container)
- Spinach
- Squash
- Peas (Sugar Snap, Snow Peas, English Peas)
- Cabbage
- Eggplant
- Onion (Green or Scallion)
- Beets

There are more container plant possibilities than I can list in this short gardening guide. Though perhaps not common, I've seen avocado trees and cantaloupes grown in containers. Just remember, some plants will need more care than others. A cactus is pretty self-sufficient; roses require a little more time and effort. And, certain plants will grow better in your region than others. When deciding what to plant, it's a good idea to take a walk around your neighborhood and note what's growing and what's growing well.

Those are the plants you probably want to use.

CHAPTER 4
GOING TO GROUND:
GETTING YOUR PLANTS GROWING

Once you've selected your plants, the real fun begins: planting. There are three methods to get your plants growing: transplanting, seed-starting, and direct sow.

Transplanting

Transplanting provides instant gratification as the end product is an immediate garden. When buying plants, choose those that have minimal (if any) blooms and avoid vegetable plants that are already producing. Plant leaves should be green and perky, not yellow, brown, or wilted. Steer clear of clearance plants whose leaves are usually yellow, brown, and wilted; these poor plants have been heavily neglected and probably won't survive a transplant.

If possible, buy plants from a local nursery rather than a large wholesaler like Home Depot or WalMart. Local greenhouses are more likely to carry plant varieties that grow well in your region, and their plants have been properly watered, fertilized, and are, generally, better cared for.

To Transplant a Plant:

1. Cover the planter's drainage ports with an object that will allow water to drain while keeping soil in the pot. A small rock, a shard from a broken planter, or a piece of netting works well.

   Some gardeners advise putting a layer of rocks at the bottom of a planter for better drainage. But, others admonish that this diminishes the plant's growing space and can damage its roots. I use both methods. If a planter needs extra drainage or weight, I'll use the rocks. Otherwise, I'll skip that step.

2. Partially fill the planter with potting soil to the point where if you set your plant on the top of the soil, the root or soil bulb of the plant will be about one-and-a-half to two inches from the top of the planter.

3. Turn the plant upside down and gently remove it from its current container. Likely, the plant will slide out easily. If not, lightly tap the bottom of the container or gently squeeze the sides. Never yank a plant out by its stem. Gently loosen the plant's root ball. This will encourage the plant's roots to grow outward and better anchor the plant.

   If the plant's soil is dry, water and wait thirty minutes before transplanting. If the plant is too dry, its soil will crumble when you remove it from the container, and the root system could be damaged.

4. Place the plant in the container and finish filling the pot with soil, gently tamping in the soil around the plant. The planter should be filled to within an inch of its rim. Give the plant a good drink of water when you're done.

Seed Starting

Seed packets are generally cheaper than plants, and there are a lot of seeds in a packet. You can also find plant varieties in seed form that may be hard to find at your local nursery (just make sure the plant will grow in your region!).

Seeds can (and should) be started indoors weeks ahead of the last frost. Some plants have to be started indoors, such as tomatoes, peppers, and herbs. The directions on your seed packet will let you know if the plant should be seed-started and when to start planting.

To Start Seeds Indoors:

1. Fill seed-starting containers or trays with moistened potting soil to a quarter inch from the top. Seed starting kits can be purchased at most garden supply stores. You can also use an egg carton or reuse the small, black plastic flats your nursery plants came in.

2. Place two to three seeds on top of the soil and cover with a fine layer of dirt to the planting depth recommended on the seed packet.

3. Water your new plantings. To keep seeds from washing out, use a spray bottle instead of a watering can. It's important to keep seeds consistently moist but not soggy. Too dry and the seeds won't germinate. Too wet and the seeds will rot.

   For faster germination, you can cover your containers with clear plastic. Most seed starting kits include a plastic topper with the tray. You can also use Saran (or some other brand) plastic wrap.

4. Keep plants in a warm place. The tops of televisions or other appliances work well.

5. Once plants start sprouting, move them to a place with good sunlight, like a south-facing window. If you live in a place that doesn't get good sunlight (like me), you may have to invest in grow lights. If your new plants are too leggy, don't develop

secondary (true) leaves, or flop over and start growing sideways, they're not receiving enough sunlight.

6. You'll need to thin your plants once the seedlings' develop their true leaves by choosing your favorite seedling and removing others that aren't. Yes, this seems mean, and I have to deal with a certain amount of guilt each time I do it, but plants need room to grow, and the seedlings will eventually strangle each other if you allow all of them to develop.

   Thinning is easier to accomplish when soil is drier, so thin before you water. Don't wait until the seedlings are too big, or their roots will become intertwined, and you risk damaging your intended plant when you remove the others. A good rule of thumb: if the plants' leaves are touching each other, it's time to thin.

   If you do wait too long, rather than pull the extraneous seedlings, cut them off at the base of their stem.

7. Once outdoor temperatures are warm enough to sustain outdoor plants, you'll have to harden off your seedlings. This just means "get them used to living outside."

   Start by leaving seedlings outdoors, in a sheltered, sunny (but not scorching) area, for 3-4 hours. Gradually increase their outdoor exposure each by a few hours each day. After 7-10 days, the seedlings are ready for transplant.

Direct Sow

This is the easiest means of planting but also the most likely to fail. If seeds fail to sprout after four weeks, replant.

Some seeds have to be directly sown. Corn generally doesn't transplant well, and peas are best direct sown. Basically, if the seed pack directions state to sow the seed an inch or more deep, seeds should probably be directly sown.

1. Fill planter with potting soil to within an inch of the top of the pot.

2. Sow seeds according to the depth recommended by the package.

3. The rules for watering directly sown seeds are the same as seed-starters. Soil needs to be moist but not soaking to prevent seed rot and encourage germination.

4. Sown seedlings will also need to be thinned when they're 2"-3" tall. It's better to trim the extraneous plants at the base of their stem rather than pull them.

All plants and seeds come with specific planting instructions on their labels or packets. These guides will let you know when to plant, how to plant, how to water, how much sun the plant needs, and time to harvest (if you're planting vegetables). Follow these instructions to the letter, and you will be rewarded with happy, healthy plants. Ignore them, and you risk maladapted plants bent on your container garden's destruction.

CHAPTER 5
PLANT RX:
GROWING HEALTHY PLANTS
(& KEEPING THEM THAT WAY)

Your containers have been purchased; your plants are bought and potted. Now comes the tricky part: keeping your plants alive. Consistently watering and fertilizing your plants and promptly dealing with any garden pests or plant diseases will go a long way in ensuring a healthy container garden.

Watering Your Container Garden

Though it may sound simple, watering can be confusing at times. When I bought a strawberry plant for my container garden, I asked the nursery attendant who rang up my purchase how much I should water my new plant. She answered, "An inch of water every other day until the plant is producing; then water every day."

This sounded like sage advice until I got home and realized I didn't know what she meant by "an inch of water." An inch of water on top of the soil? Until the soil was damp down to an inch? An inch of water from my watering can? What if rained that day? How did that count against my inch?

Different plants need different amounts of water. Cucumbers require far more water than peppers. The same plants can also require different amounts of water depending on climate, the time of year, the point in the plant's growth cycle, and the size or material of the container the plant is growing in. Unfortunately, there is no hard and fast rule for watering container plants. The following list will help you gage how much and when to water.

- ■ The general rule of thumb? Stick your finger an inch deep into the plant's soil. The soil should feel moist. If the soil is soaking, you're watering too much. If the soil is dry, the plant needs to be watered.

- ■ When watering, water slowly. Too much water too quickly will drain straight through the pot and leave the root ball dry. Slowly fill the pot once and let the water sink in. A small amount of water should leak through the drainage ports. If this doesn't happen, slowly add more water to the plant until it does.

- ■ Routinely check drainage ports on your containers. If the holes are blocked, you risk drowning your plant.

- ■ If the plant's leaves are turning yellow, you're overwatering the plant. If they're drying up or turning brown, you're underwatering the plant.

- ■ Plants tend to droop a bit in the afternoon when the weather is hot. Don't panic and know your plants may not need water. Check the soil: if it's damp, the plant is fine. If a plant is wilted in the cooler morning, however, water immediately.

- If vegetable plants are producing or the weather is hot, you'll probably need to water more than once per day. Ditto for flowering plants and large plants in small pots.

- Be wary of self-watering pots, and if you plan on going this route, invest in a good system. It's never a good idea to leave plants in standing water.

- Small, home drip irrigation systems work well for watering plants, but they can be a little pricy and require access to an outdoor spigot.

- The type of container you use will partially dictate the plant's watering schedule. Smaller pots will need to be watered more often than larger pots. Porous planters, like terra cotta pots, will need to be watered more often than glazed planters.

- Soil moisture meters can help take some of the guesswork out of watering. But, these devices can be unreliable, particularly right after a plant has been fertilized.

Fertilizing Your Container Garden

This is a step new gardeners, and even seasoned gardeners, often skip. I'm really not sure why. Given the container garden's restricted environment, the plants sap the soil's nutrients quickly, and the soil cannot replenish them. As well, each time you water, vital nutrients are washed out of the soil and through the container's drainage port.

Plants will starve without proper nutrition. Most vegetable plants won't even produce without continually fertilizing the soil. As the gardener, it's your job to feed your plants, and it can be done in a few different ways:

- You can mix slow release fertilizer in with your potting soil. This will help feed your plant from 2-4 months. Just make sure the potting soil you chose isn't already fertilized (many are).

- Water-soluble fertilizer can be added to water every week or two to give your plants an extra boost. Some water-soluble varieties can even be sprayed directly on plant leaves for instant nutrition.

- Different plants require different types of fertilizer. Flowering plants like lots of nitrogen. Vegetable plants don't. Be sure to read and follow all package instructions.

- There are lots of organic fertilizers out there. If you're particularly adventurous, you can invest in a countertop composter and create your own. Coffee grounds are great for acid-loving plants. Eggshells can be used to add calcium into the soil.

Pest Control

There are few things more frustrating than waiting weeks to harvest fresh produce, finally going out one morning to pick a newly ripened pepper, and finding a large hole chewed in the fruit by a particularly soulless caterpillar. Luckily, pests aren't often as large of a problem in a container garden as they are in a traditional garden, but you still need to be vigilant and deal with pest problems as soon as you spot them. You can limit pests or even eliminate them through the following practices:

- Start each growing season with clean pots and new potting soil. Never, ever, ever reuse potting soil. The soil's nutrients are gone, and many pests like to lay their eggs in the old soil. The larvae lie in wait until spring and take the first opportunity to destroy your plants or wipe out your crop.

- Keep your plants clean. Pick off dead leaves and spent blooms. Remove fallen foliage from the base of your plant. Pests love to hide beneath all those dead leaves.

- Remove large pests, such as caterpillars or slugs, from your plants. You can destroy them by dropping them into a bowl of soapy water. If you're against this type of slaughter, be sure to relocate these visitors far from your garden, or they'll be back.

- Small pests, like aphids, can be removed with a spray bottle of soapy water. Actually, this eco-friendly mix deters quite a few pests. Mix ½ teaspoon of dish soap per quart of water.

- Not all bugs are bad bugs, and many can help you keep less desirable bugs away. Lacewings eat aphids and whiteflies. Ground beetles eat snails. Spiders eat pests of all kinds.

Plant Diseases

Plants can get sick. They're subject to wilt, rot, mildew, and fungus, especially if you live in a humid environment. Consider:

- If plants are properly watered and adequately fertilized, the chance of plant disease drops dramatically. Healthy plants, like healthy people, are better able to withstand infections.

- Always keep your garden clean and remove infected leaves, dead leaves, and spent blooms. Use clean garden tools, especially pruning shears.

- Water plants below leaves and blooms to discourage mold or mildew from forming.

- If a plant is badly infested, remove it from your garden lest it infect your other plants. Consider disposing containers that have held infected plants.

- Adding a few teaspoons of baking soda to your soapy water mixture and spraying plant leaves can cure many fungal diseases. Instead of baking soda, you can also use apple cider vinegar or mouthwash.

CONCLUSION

You've made it to the end! Hazah! You now know the basics of container gardening. You've outlined a plan that will provide you with the best garden for you. You know what containers you're going to buy and why they'll work best for your garden. You know what soil you're going to use (potting soil, right?). You know what plants to look for and how to care for them.

Before we part, I want to leave you with a final bit of information. You may recall my mentioning that gardens are greatly affected by the region they grow in. You probably recall this because I mentioned it several times. In this short guide, I can't address every region's unique gardening needs. But, I can provide you with a list of your local places that can. Here it is:

- Local greenhouses and nurseries
- Local farmer's markets
- Your city's agricultural extension office
- Local agricultural schools
- Local gardening clubs

These resources will know what plants grow best in your region and when to plant them. If a particular garden pest or disease is making the rounds, they'll know about it, and they'll know how to help you fight it. Your city's agricultural extension and any local agricultural schools may offer community classes on composting, organic gardening, region-specific pest prevention, or other regional gardening topics. All of these places love to talk gardening and are very generous with their time in helping newbie gardeners.

I hope you've enjoyed this container gardening guide, and I hope it's provided you with a wealth of ideas for your own container garden. It's now time for you to go out and get planting.

Good luck and happy gardening.